Chimpanzees

by Karen Kane
photographs by Gerry Ellis

Early Bird Nature Books

Lerner Publications Company • Minneapolis

Many thanks to the men and women who have dedicated their lives to the protection and conservation of the chimpanzee. Our world would be poorer without your passion for this endangered species. *—KK*

My thanks to Jane Goodall for her caring and commitment, enriching the lives of chimps and all creatures, and bringing us closer to understanding our fellow earthlings. Also, a personal note of gratitude for her sharing the private world of the chimps in Gombe Stream with me. *—GE*

Additional photographs are reproduced with permission from: © Charles V. Angelo/Photo Researchers, Inc., p. 18; © Tim Davis/Photo Researchers, Inc., p. 25; © Mark Newman/Photo Researchers, Inc., p. 28; © Wendy Dennis/Visuals Unlimited, p. 30; © Tom McHugh/Photo Researchers, Inc., p. 31; © Susan Kuklin/Photo Researchers, Inc., p. 42.

Lerner Publications Company
A division of Lerner Publishing Group
241 First Avenue North
Minneapolis, MN 55401 U.S.A

Website address: www.lernerbooks.com

Library of Congress Cataloging-in-Publication Data

Kane, Karen.
Chimpanzees / by Karen Kane ; photographs by Gerry Ellis.
p. cm. — (Early bird nature books)
Includes index.
Contents: Chimpanzees are not monkeys—Chimpanzees at home—All day long—Chimp families—Chimp talk—The little ones—The world outside.
ISBN: 0–8225–2418–X (lib. bdg. : alk. paper)
1. Chimpanzees—Juvenile literature. [1. Chimpanzees.]
I. Ellis, Gerry, ill. II. Title. III. Series.
QL737.P96K255 2005
599.885—dc22 2003027285

Manufactured in the United States of America
1 2 3 4 5 6 - JR - 10 09 08 07 06 05

Contents

Chimpanzees live in western and central Africa. The red areas show where chimpanzees live.

Be a Word Detective

Can you find these words as you read about the chimpanzee's life? Be a detective and try to figure out what they mean. You can turn to the glossary on page 46 for help.

community
endangered
extinct
habitats
knuckle walking
nest
nurses
omnivores
primates
rain forests
social grooming
territory

Chapter 1

Chimpanzees are not monkeys. But chimpanzees and monkeys belong to the same group of animals. What is this group called?

Chimpanzees Are Not Monkeys!

Chimpanzees are animals that look a little bit like people. Maybe you have seen chimpanzees at a zoo. People often call them "chimps" for short.

Chimps belong to a group of animals called primates (PRY-mayts). Monkeys, chimpanzees, and people are all primates. Primates have two arms, two legs, 10 fingers, and 10 toes. Primates can hold on to things with their hands and their feet.

A chimp's foot (left) *looks like a hand. The big toe can even grip things like a thumb can.*

Chimps are part of a special group of primates called apes. Gorillas and orangutans are also apes. Apes are very smart. Apes are also bigger than other primates. An ape's arms are longer than its legs. Most primates have tails. But apes do not.

Orangutans (above) *and mountain gorillas* (right) *are closely related to chimpanzees.*

Chimps walk on the ground when they travel long distances through the forest.

A chimp usually walks with both its arms and its legs. The chimp curls its fingers and leans on its knuckles. This way of walking is called knuckle walking.

This chimp looks short when it is sitting on the ground. But if the chimp stood on its legs, its head would come up to the man's waist or chest.

Chimpanzees are about 3 to 4 feet tall. That is about the same size as a five-year-old person. But chimps are heavy and strong. A big male chimp can weigh almost 200 pounds. Female chimpanzees are smaller than males.

Chimps have dark hair covering their bodies. They have pink or dark skin on their faces. Many chimpanzees' ears stick out from their heads.

Chimpanzees do not have hair on their hands, feet, ears, or faces. But most chimps have some hair around their mouths.

Chapter 2

The scientific name for the chimpanzee is Pan troglodytes. *Where do chimps live?*

Chimpanzees at Home

Chimpanzees live in central and western Africa. They live in forests and grasslands. The areas where chimps live are called their habitats (HAB-uh-tats).

Rain forests have more kinds of plants and animals than any other place on Earth. Scientists have learned about only some of the living things in rain forests.

The forests chimpanzees live in are called tropical rain forests. Tropical rain forests are usually very hot and wet. They stay warm all year long. There are no cold winters there.

Chimps spend a lot of time in trees. These chimps are sitting in a fig tree. The round fruits growing on its branches are figs.

A rain forest is made up of many different sizes of trees. Lots of short bushes cover the ground. Thick vines dangle from trees. The ground is shady. But the sun shines brightly near the tops of the trees. Many kinds of flowers and fruits grow there.

Chimps are good at climbing trees. They use their long arms to swing from branch to branch. And they can jump from tree to tree.

A chimp's strong arms help it move around in the trees.

Lots of animals, plants, birds, and insects live with chimpanzees in the rain forests. Birds, butterflies, insects, and monkeys move through the trees. Other animals, such as mice, snakes, and elephants, live on the ground. Fish swim in the streams.

Leopards sit in the trees of the rain forest. They wait for animals like chimps to come by. Leopards hunt and eat chimpanzees.

Chapter 3

These chimps live together in the same group. What is a large group of chimps called?

Chimp Families

Chimpanzees live in large groups. A large group of chimps is called a community. As many as 100 chimps live in a community.

Older male chimps are the leaders of their community. They protect the community from dangerous animals, such as leopards.

The chimps in a community share a big area of land. This area is the community's territory. A territory is like a neighborhood. A community does not like to share its territory with chimpanzees from other communities. But it will share its territory with other kinds of animals, such as monkeys.

Sometimes the chimps in a community form small groups. The small groups travel together. A group may be made up of only males or only females. It may be made up of only mothers and babies. Or it may be a group of young chimps from different families.

Chimpanzees often travel in small groups. But the groups are still part of the community.

Chapter 4

This chimp is eating the leaves off a tree. What else do chimps do during the day?

All Day Long

Chimpanzees do pretty much the same things every day. As they move through the forest, chimps eat, play, rest, and sleep.

Sometimes chimps just sit together. They clean sticks, dirt, and leaves out of each other's hair. This is called social grooming. Chimpanzees spend quite a bit of their day grooming each other.

Chimps groom the other chimps in their small group.

Figs make a great meal for chimps.

Chimps spend a lot of time looking for food. Chimpanzees are omnivores (AHM-nih-vohrz). Omnivores are animals who eat both plants and animals. Some of a chimp's favorite foods are fruits and leaves. Chimps also eat seeds, tree bark, plant stems, flowers, and honey. Birds' eggs, ants, and insects are tasty. Even small monkeys and pigs make good meals.

A community of chimps find a place in the rain forest where there is lots of good food. They stay there until the food is gone. Sometimes they stay in one place for many days.

Scientists think that chimpanzees eat more than 200 different kinds of plants!

When the food is gone, the chimps move. They go to another part of the rain forest where there are more good things to eat. But they remember where they found food before. After a while, the food will grow back in those places. The chimps go back to these places to get more good food to eat.

This chimp has found some insects to eat.

To open hard objects, chimps pound on them with rocks.

Chimps use tools to help them get or eat their food. Rocks and sticks make good tools. Chimps use rocks to break the shells of nuts and seeds. Then they can eat the tasty inside parts. A chimp will poke a stick into a hole in a mound and wait for insects to climb up the stick. Then the chimp puts the stick in its mouth and licks off the insects. Yummy!

If a chimpanzee wants a drink, it may crumple up some leaves and soak them in water like a sponge. Then the chimp will suck the water from the leaves.

Chimps use tools in other ways too. They use leaves and small twigs to brush dirt off their hair.

Adult chimps teach younger chimps how to use tools.

Chimps make nests during the day if they are tired or it is very hot.

Every night, each chimpanzee makes a nest to sleep in. Chimpanzees usually make nests high in the treetops. This keeps chimps safe from animals that might want to hurt them.

A chimpanzee will climb up into a tree. Then the chimp pulls branches, leaves, and sticks together to make a nest. The chimpanzee curls up on top of the nest and falls asleep.

Chapter 5

Chimps make lots of noises. What kinds of sounds can chimps make?

Chimp Talk

Chimps are active and noisy. They talk to each other by making sounds or movements. Each chimp has a different voice, just like people.

Scientists have learned that chimpanzees make about 30 different sounds. Chimps hoot, shriek, scream, and roar. They also grunt and bark. Sometimes they are so loud that they can be heard from half a mile away!

If chimps are far away from each other, they talk with a sound called a pant-hoot. A pant-hoot sounds like "hoo, hoo, hoo," with a breath after each "hoo."

This baby chimp seems excited. What noises do you think it is making?

Chimpanzees make sounds for many different reasons. They make sounds if they are angry, happy, excited, or sad. They make sounds if they don't understand something. They make sounds if they find food. They make sounds if other chimpanzees are in their territory or if they see something dangerous. And they make sounds to say hello to one another.

When chimps play or greet each other, they make friendly noises. When chimps are angry, they roar and scream.

This chimp is telling another animal to stay away.

When chimps are angry, they do many things. They hoot and holler. They slap the ground with their hands. Sometimes chimps throw rocks, sticks, and dirt. They also wave branches and chase each other or other animals.

Chimpanzees also talk by making faces. When a chimpanzee looks like it is smiling, it is probably frightened. And when a chimpanzee opens its mouth wide and round and shows its teeth, the chimp is angry.

Chapter 6

Young chimps have white hair on their bottoms and pink skin. How much does a chimp weigh when it is born?

The Little Ones

When a female chimp is about 12 years old, she will have her first baby. A baby chimpanzee weighs about 4 pounds when it is born. That is about half the size of a newborn human baby.

When a mother chimp is sitting or sleeping, she holds her baby in her arms. The baby nurses. Nursing is drinking mother's milk.

Chimps nurse until they are four or five years old.

The mother protects her newborn baby. A baby chimp clings to its mother's belly when she walks through the forest or climbs trees. When the baby chimp is about six months old, it learns how to ride on its mother's back. It also explores near her.

A baby chimp and its mother sleep in the same nest until the baby is four or five years old. By then, the mother chimp might have another baby.

A mother chimp talks to her baby.

Mother chimpanzees love to play with their babies. A mother chimp will let her baby crawl all over her and even jump on her! She will lie on her back and dangle the baby from her arms. Then she will tickle it. Some mothers playfully poke their babies with tiny twigs. Other mothers chase their babies. Chimps also cuddle their babies and groom their hair.

After about four or five years, the young chimp is old enough to live on its own. But most of the time, it stays near its mom. Brothers, sisters, and other babies from the group look after each other. They play together and eat together.

Older brothers and sisters take care of the new babies in their family.

Mother chimpanzees and their families stay close to each other for much of their lives. A young chimpanzee will live in its mother's community for up to 10 years. Then female chimps sometimes leave their community to live in another one. But male chimps usually stay in the same community. Most chimps live about 45 years.

A chimp family walks across a stream.

Chapter 7

There are few places left in the world where chimps can live. What is happening to the chimpanzee's habitats?

The World Outside

Chimpanzees are endangered. This means that there are few chimps left in the world. There are many reasons why chimps are endangered. The most important reason is that chimpanzees' habitats are being destroyed.

People are cutting down the trees in the rain forests. Some people need wood to make fires to cook their food. Other people sell wood to make furniture and other things. People also cut down the forests to make room to build homes and farms.

Trees are cut down to build roads through parts of the rain forest.

Some people make money by selling baby chimps at markets. But it is illegal to own or sell wild chimps in most countries.

When trees are cut down, chimpanzees must move to places where there are still trees. If other chimpanzees already live there, the new chimps are not welcomed. The new chimps may be attacked and killed by the other chimpanzees.

Some people hunt chimpanzees for food. People also kill chimpanzees if they think that the chimps are taking food from their farms.

Many people are working hard to protect chimpanzees. Some countries in Africa have made parks where chimpanzees can be safe. People are not allowed to build homes or farms in these places.

In the parks, people leave out food for chimps. As the chimps eat, people can watch and study them.

Some chimpanzees do not live in the wild forests. They live in zoos, in animal reserves, or with people who study them. People have taught some of these chimps to use sign language. Sign language is a way of using your hands to let others know what you mean. People who cannot hear use sign language. Some chimps have learned more than 200 signs.

Chimps cannot speak like people can. But some chimps have learned sign language.

Dr. Jane Goodall (center) *has been studying chimps for nearly 50 years. She works hard to save the chimpanzee and its habitat.*

Scientists have been studying chimps for many years. This helps them to understand how chimps live and what they eat. Knowing these things will help people to save chimps from becoming extinct (ehk-STINGKT). When a kind of animal is extinct, there are no more left in the world.

Chimpanzees are amazing animals. People need to learn more about chimps. Then it will be easier to keep chimps safe.

A NOTE TO ADULTS

On Sharing a Book

As you know, adults greatly influence a child's attitude toward reading. When a child sees you read, or when you share a book with a child, you're sending a message that reading is important. Show the child that reading a book together is important to you. Find a comfortable, quiet place. Turn off the television and limit other distractions, such as telephone calls.

Be prepared to start slowly. Take turns reading parts of this book. Stop and talk about what you're reading. Talk about the photographs. You may find that much of the shared time is spent discussing just a few pages. This discussion time is valuable for both of you, so don't move through the book too quickly. If the child begins to lose interest, stop reading. Continue sharing the book at another time. When you do pick up the book again, be sure to revisit the parts you have already read. Most importantly, enjoy the book!

Be a Vocabulary Detective

You will find a word list on page 5. Words selected for this list are important to the understanding of the topic of this book. Encourage the child to be a word detective and search for the words as you read the book together. Talk about what the words mean and how they are used in the sentence. Do any of these words have more than one meaning? You will find these words defined in a glossary on page 46.

What about Questions?

Use questions to make sure the child understands the information in this book. Here are some suggestions:

> What did this paragraph tell us? What does this picture show? What do you think we'll learn about next? How are chimpanzees like other primates? How are they different? What do chimpanzees eat? Could a chimpanzee live in your backyard? Why/Why not? How long does a young chimpanzee live with its mother? How do people cause problems for chimpanzees? What do you think it's like being a chimpanzee? What is your favorite part of the book? Why?

If the child has questions, don't hesitate to respond with questions of your own, such as What do *you* think? Why? What is it that you don't know? If the child can't remember certain facts, turn to the index.

Introducing the Index

The index is an important learning tool. It helps readers get information quickly without searching throughout the whole book. Turn to the index on page 47. Choose an entry, such as *eating*, and ask the child to use the index to find out what foods chimpanzees eat. Repeat this exercise with as many entries as you like. Ask the child to point out the differences between an index and a glossary. (The index helps readers find information quickly, while the glossary tells readers what words mean.)

Where in the World?

Many plants and animals found in the Early Bird Nature Books series live in parts of the world other than the United States. Encourage the child to find the places mentioned in this book on a world map or globe. Take time to talk about climate, terrain, and how you might live in such places.

All the World in Metric!

Although our monetary system is in metric units (based on multiples of 10), the United States is one of the few countries in the world that does not use the metric system of measurement. Here are some conversion activities you and the child can do using a calculator:

WHEN YOU KNOW:	MULTIPLY BY:	TO FIND:
miles	1.609	kilometers
feet	0.3048	meters
inches	2.54	centimeters
gallons	3.785	liters
tons	0.907	metric tons
pounds	0.454	kilograms

Activities

Go to the website for the Jane Goodall Institute (http://www.janegoodall.org) to learn more about chimpanzees.

Visit a zoo to see chimpanzees. How are chimpanzees in the zoo similar to other primates, such as monkeys? How are they different?

Pretend that you are a chimpanzee. How do you walk? What sounds do you make?

Glossary

community: a large group of chimpanzees who live together

endangered: in danger of dying out

extinct (ehk-STINGKT): no members of a kind of animal are still living

habitats (HAB-uh-tats): the areas where a kind of animal can live and grow

knuckle walking: leaning on the knuckles of the hands while walking

nest: a bed that chimps make out of branches, sticks, and leaves

nurses: drinks mother's milk

omnivores (AHM-nih-vohrz): animals who eat both plants and animals

primates (PRY-mayts): animals who have bodies shaped like human bodies. Monkeys, chimpanzees, and people are all primates.

rain forests: warm, thick forests where a lot of rain falls

social grooming: taking care of another chimp by removing sticks, dirt, and leaves from its hair

territory: the area where a group of chimpanzees lives

Index

Pages listed in **bold** type refer to photographs.

About the Author

Author, naturalist, and conservationist Karen Kane is an active participant in promoting the understanding and appreciation of Earth's wilds. Widely traveled, she has studied wildlife and the environment for much of her life. Her interest in the natural world has been heightened by observing wild animals in their habitats on all seven continents. Karen has written three other books, including *Mountain Gorillas.* She lives in Portland, Oregon, where she hikes, bikes, skis, paddles, and sails.

About the Photographer

Gerry Ellis communicates his passion for the natural world through his award-winning wildlife and nature photography. A dedicated naturalist, he has explored the world for two decades, visiting every continent in his quest to experience nature in its wildest and purest forms. His interest in primates has taken him to remote areas of Africa, where he has worked with chimpanzees and mountain gorillas, and to Borneo, where he has tracked wild orangutans. Gerry's images of wildlife and nature have been awarded top honors, including several in the BBC Wildlife Photographer of the Year competition. Among his many publications are the titles *Mountain Gorillas, African Elephants, Cheetahs, Hippos, Rhinos, Slugs,* and *Zebras.*